MW00723557

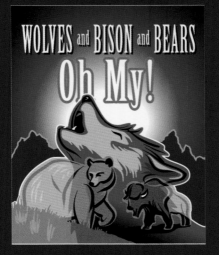

WOLVES and BISON and BEARS
Oh My!

Edited and Compiled by Carrie L. Compton

W.W.WEST

...at is man without the beasts? If all the
...easts were gone, men would die from great
...neliness of spirit, for whatever happens to
...e beasts also happens to man.

Chief Seattle

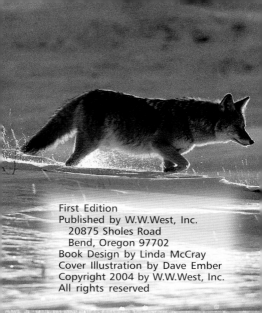

First Edition
Published by W.W.West, Inc.
  20875 Sholes Road
  Bend, Oregon 97702
Book Design by Linda McCray
Cover Illustration by Dave Ember
Copyright 2004 by W.W.West, Inc.

Photos copyright© by Photographer credited

Library Catalog data available upon request

Printed in China by C & C Offset Printing Co.

Effort has been made to attribute text to the
original source. If any required
acknowledgements have been omitted, or any
rights overlooked, it is unintentional. If notified
the publisher will be pleased to correct any
future editions.

I look forward to an America; which will not be afraid of grace and beauty, which will protect the beauty of our natural environment.

John F. Kennedy

The beauty and genius of a work of art may be reconceived, though its first expression be destroyed. But, when the last individual of a race of living things breathes no more, another heaven and another earth must pass before such a one can be again.

William Beebe, Naturalist

I would feel more optimistic about a bright future for man, if he spent less time proving that he can outwit Nature and more time respecting her.

E.B. White

A lady telephoned the ranger station demanding that a black bear be killed at once, "no one has ever been hurt or humiliated as I have been." I sent a ranger to investigate. He reported she had been feeding a big bear all morning, and tourists had been photographing the two of them.

The bear stood up as she fed him from her fingers. Visitors were taking pictures when she became distracted. The bear, thinking the show was over dropped to the ground, but, in so doing caught his claws in her dress, stripping her. She admitted to the ranger that she had not been physically injured, but none of us doubted she had been terribly humiliated. We spared the bear, however.

Horace Albright

To the Grizzly Bear
almost everything is
food, except granite.

John Muir

At the height of the fur trade, a half-million beaver a year were dying so that gentleman could wear them as hats.

Dean Krakel II

th the successful introduction of the wolf,
very animal species living in Yellowstone,
hen the park was created, is there today!

The prospect of actually seeing a wolf is "the Holy Grail of Yellowstone wildlife sightings."

Paul Schullery

There is a love of wild nature in everybody, an ancient mother-love. The wilderness, I believe, is dear to everyone though some are afraid of it.

John Muir

In wilderness I sense the miracle
of life, and behind it our scientific
accomplishments fade to trivia.

Charles A. Lindbergh

Wilderness is an anchor to windward. Knowing it is there, we can also know that we are still a rich nation, tending our resources as we should.

Clinton P Anderson, US Senator

en we who have a feeling for birds,
serve a mighty eagle, or the perfection
a tiny warbler, we see the very handiwork
the Creator Himself.

Rosalie Edge

Every year it becomes more obvious that if we humans are to allow the wilderness and its inhabitants to survive we must set aside areas—big areas, for their exclusive use.

H.R.H. Prince Philip

Mankind's true moral test, its
fundamental test, consists of its
attitude toward those who are at
its mercy—animals.

Milan Kundera

lets cage ourselves and let
the animals run free.

Steve Van Martre

Yellowstone has the largest,
and only truly wild Bison
herd, in the United States.

The Trumpeter Swan is the largest waterfowl in North America and an inhabitant of Yellowstone.

A survey of park visitors asked them to guess the weight of Black Bears (the bears were between 95 and 115 pounds), the guesses ranged from 400 to 4,000 pounds.

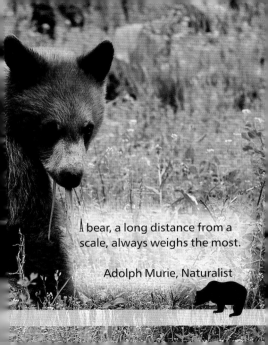

A bear, a long distance from a scale, always weighs the most.

Adolph Murie, Naturalist

ture has made her wildest patterns here, has
ought the boiling water from her greatest
epths to the peaks which bear eternal snow,
d set her masterpiece with pools like jewels.
t us respect her moods, and let the beasts
e nurtures live.

Frederick Remington

One touch of nature makes the whole world ki

William Shakespeare

What time of year do the Elk change to Moose?

Tourist question to Park Ranger

Man is the only animal that blushes—or needs to.

Mark Twain

n argument for wilderness is that we have
n ethical obligation to provide animals
with a place where they are free from the
mpingement of civilization.

Barry Lopez

ese bear (Grizzly) are a most tremendous imal; it seems that the hand of providence s been most wonderfully in our favor with spect to them, or some of us would long ce have fallen sacrifice to their ferocity.

Meriwether Lewis

Pierre Cruzatte was the first member of the expedition (Lewis and Clark), and thus the first American to get off a shot at a Grizzly. Within seconds, he became the first American to run, from what explorers came to learn was a formidable adversary when hurt and angry.

Daniel Slosberg

ife must be a race to use up everything we
ve, who exactly will win that race?

Barbara Kingsolver

I once had a sparrow alight upon my shoulder for a moment. I felt that I was more distinguished by that circumstance than I should have been by any epaulet I could have worn.

Henry David Thoreau

We can never have enough of nature.

Henry David Thoreau

When I meet a large animal face to face in the wild: I feel a kind of affection and the crazy desire to communicate, to make some kind emotional, even physical contact. After we'd stared at each other for maybe five seconds—held out one hand and took a step toward the big cat and said something ridiculous like, "Here, Kitty, Kitty." The cat was motionless, one paw up as if he wanted to shake hands.

ook a second step toward the lion. The lion
mained still, not blinking an eye. I stopped
d thought again and this time I understood
at however the big cat might secretly feel, I
yself was not quite ready to shake hands
th a mountain lion. I retreated.

Edward Abbey

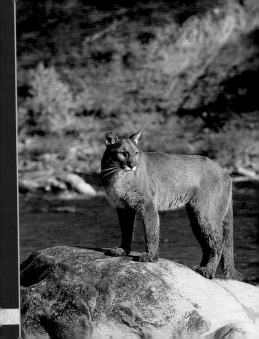

o not think any more cougars should be
lled in the park. They ought to be left alone.

President Theodore Roosevelt

Selected Bibliography

Edward Abbey (1852-1911) U.S. painter and illustrator best know for his murals in public buildings.

Horace Albright (1890-1987) One of the National Park Servi founders. He was Superintendent of Yellowstone NP and Director of the NPS.

Clinton P. Anderson (1895-1975) U.S. Senator from New Mexico.

William Beebe (1877-1962) American naturalist best known for ocean exploration.

Rosalie Edge Author. Text is from *Good Companions in Conservation: Annals of an Implacable Widow.*

James Earle Fraser (1876-1953) Designer of the U.S Buffalo (Bison) Nickel.

John F. Kennedy (1917-1963) 35th President of the United States.

Barbara Kingsolver Author. Quote is from her *Small Wonde* Essays.

Milan Kundera Czech author. Text is from *The Unbearable Lightness of Being.*

Dean Krakel II Author and Photo-Journalist.

Meriwether Lewis (1774-1809) Explorer with William Clark the Northwest Territories to the Pacific Ocean.

Charles A. Lindbergh (1902-1974) Engineer, aviator, and the first person to fly solo across the Atlantic Ocean.

Barry Lopez Author. Text is from *Crossing Open Ground* 1983.

nn Muir (1838-1914) Conservationist, naturalist and
explorer who was instrumental in establishing Yosemite as
a national park.

R.H Prince Phillip Duke of Edinburgh quoted during a visit
to Yellowstone.

ederick Remington (1861-1909) U.S. painter and sculptor
famous for his works of the American West.

eodore Roosevelt (1859-1919) 26th President of the United
States. He was an avid outdoorsman and conservation
advocate.

ul Schullery Author of nature works, including *Mountain
Time* and *Lewis and Clark Among the Grizzlies.*

ief Seattle (1786-1866) A leader of the tribes in the Puget
Sound, Washington area. The most frequently quoted
Native American.

. Seuss (1904-1991) Theodore Seuss Geisel, writer and
illustrator of children's books.

lliam Shakespeare (1564-1616) English poet and
playwright. Quote is from *Troilus and Cressida.*

enry David Thoreau (1817-1862) U.S philosopher and author
who lived close to nature.

ark Twain (1835-1919) Samuel Clemens, U.S. author of
such classic stories as, *Tom Sawyer* and *Innocents Abroad.*

eve Van Martre Author. Text is from *The Earth Speaks*
1983

B. White (1899-1985) U.S. author best known for his
children's stories, including *Charlotte's Web.*

Photo Credits

John L. Hinderman Copyright ©

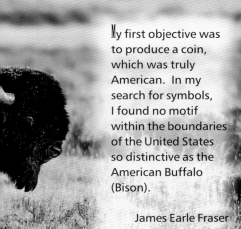

My first objective was to produce a coin, which was truly American. In my search for symbols, I found no motif within the boundaries of the United States so distinctive as the American Buffalo (Bison).

James Earle Fraser

And the turtles, of course—
all the turtles are free.

As turtles and, maybe, all
creatures should be.

Dr Seuss, *Yertle the Turtle*